THE WORLD'S TOP TEN

CAVES

Neil Morris

Illustrated by Vanessa Card

Chrysalis Children's Books

Words in **bold** are explained in the glossary
on pages 30–31.

This edition published in 2003 by
Chrysalis Children's Books
The Chrysalis Building, Bramley Road,
London W10 6SP

Copyright in this format © Chrysalis Books PLC
Text copyright © Neil Morris
Illustrations copyright © Vanessa Card
Maps copyright © Robin Carter, Wildlife Art Agency

ISBN 1 84138 480 1

British Library Cataloguing in Publication Data for this book
is available from the British Library.

Editor: Maria O'Neill
Designer: Dawn Apperley
Picture Researcher: Diana Morris
Consultant: Elizabeth M Lewis

Printed in China By Imago

Picture acknowledgements:
Bryan & Cherry Alexander Photography: 28b.
J Allan Cash: 5t. Bruce Coleman Collection: 10
MPL Fogden. James Davis Photography: 28t.
Andy Eavis: 19. Eisriesenwelt GmbH: 12.
Explorer: 15 JM Labatt, 22 P Roy.
Chris Howes: 5b, 12, 16, 17.
Peter Morris Photography: 20, 21.
Still Pictures: 29t Bojan Brecelj.
Waitomo Caves Museum Society: 27.
Tony Waltham Geophotos: 18, 23, 24, 25, 29b.
Zefa: 8 Fritz Breig, 9, 11, 14, 26.

Contents

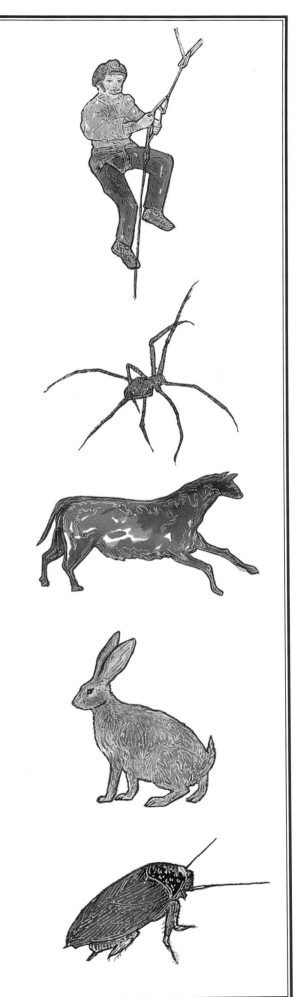

What is a cave?

A cave is a hollow space in the Earth's **crust**. Some caves are narrow, natural tunnels that run just below the surface. Other, bigger caves are kilometres long, forming deep holes in the Earth's outer layer of rocks.

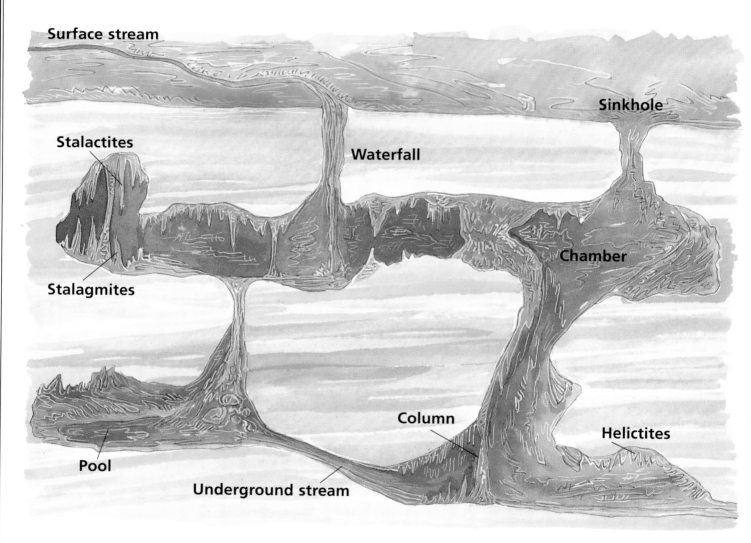

Surface stream

Stalactites

Waterfall

Sinkhole

Chamber

Stalagmites

Column

Helictites

Pool

Underground stream

How caves form

Most of the world's caves are found in limestone regions. Limestone is a soft rock that is dissolved by weak acid. Rainwater is a weak acid because it contains **carbon dioxide**. It absorbs carbon dioxide as the rain falls through the air and sinks through soil.

Over thousands of years, rainwater slowly eats away at cracks in limestone rocks. The cracks grow wider, making holes and then wide passages. This lets even more water flow through the rock, so that underground rivers form and carve out bigger caves.

4

Different types

Limestone is one of the most common types of rock on Earth. Most of the amazing caves described in this book were formed in limestone, and they are located in many different parts of the world. But there are other types of caves, too. Caves on the seashore are made by the sea crashing against rocky cliffs, widening cracks and finally creating holes. Caves also form in ice and in the **molten** rock thrown out by volcanoes.

A river flows through the entrance of Sof Omar Cave, in the Ethiopian highlands of East Africa. This huge cave has been worn away in a limestone cliff.

Amazing caves

In this book we take a look at some of the world's most amazing caves. They have been chosen to show different, fascinating features. Some are very big, others very deep. Some caves have beautiful natural **formations**, while others were decorated by humans thousands of years ago. Some caves are home to unusual creatures, others contain the remains of **prehistoric** animals.

This small narrow cave in South Wales is popular with cavers. It is easy to see why caving is such a tough, exciting sport. But it can be dangerous, especially when rain raises the water level.

5

The most amazing caves

This map shows the location of the ten amazing caves chosen for this book. Four of them are on the continent of Europe, three are in North America, two in Australasia and one in Asia. There are many caves on the other continents, too, as you can see on pages 28 and 29.

There is evidence that early humans used caves for shelter at least 500 000 years ago. Today, we find out about caves and their history through the work of scientists who study them. Cave scientists are called speleologists. Some people enjoy exploring caves as a sport, which we call caving, potholing or spelunking. Many people visit and enjoy caves simply as tourists.

Ten amazing caves

Blue Grotto	Capri, Italy
Carlsbad Caverns	New Mexico, USA
Eisriesenwelt	Werfen, Austria
Lascaux	Dordogne, France
Lava Beds	California, USA
Mammoth Cave	Kentucky, USA
Naracoorte	South Australia, Australia
Pierre-Saint-Martin	Pyrenees, France
Sarawak Chamber	Borneo, Malaysia
Waitomo	North Island, New Zealand

NORTH AMERICA

Lava Beds ■

■ Mammoth Cave

Carlsbad ■
Caverns

ATLANTIC OCEAN

SOUTH AMERICA

PACIFIC OCEAN

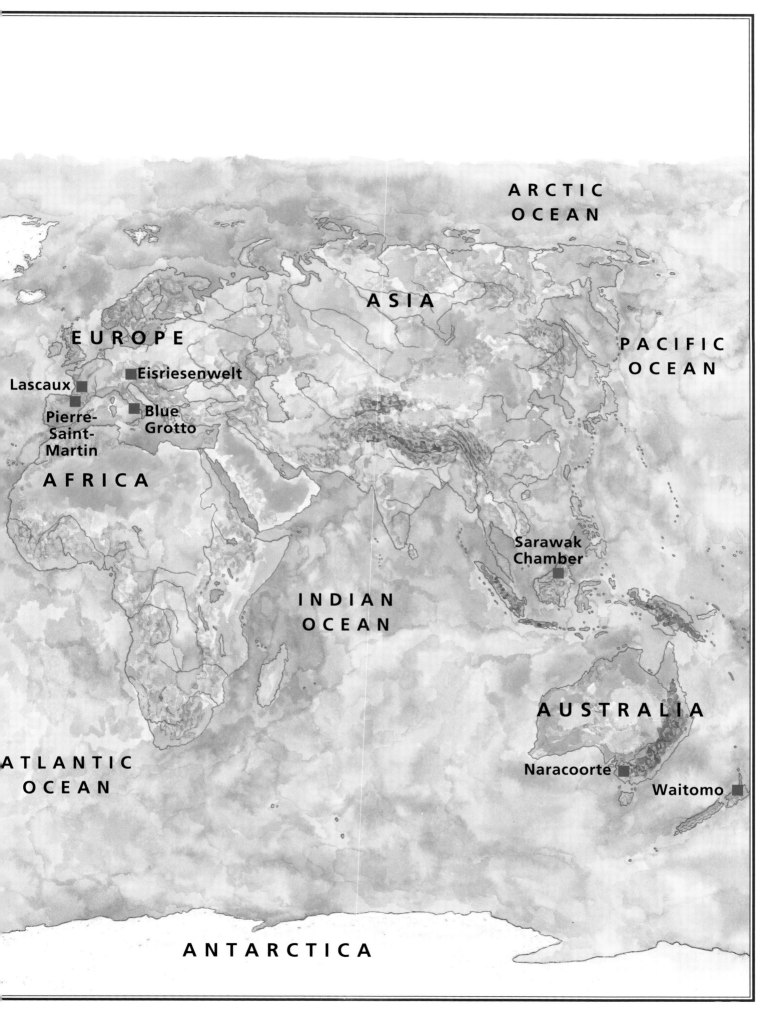

ARCTIC
OCEAN

ASIA

PACIFIC
OCEAN

EUROPE

Eisriesenwelt

Lascaux

Pierre-
Saint-
Martin

Blue
Grotto

AFRICA

Sarawak
Chamber

INDIAN
OCEAN

AUSTRALIA

ATLANTIC
OCEAN

Naracoorte

Waitomo

ANTARCTICA

Blue Grotto

This beautiful sea cave is on the island of Capri, off the coast of southern Italy. Capri is more than 6 kilometres long, less than 3 kilometres wide and 589 metres above the sea at its highest point. The Blue Grotto is Capri's most famous cave. The term 'grotto' is used to describe a small, beautiful cave.

Limestone island

Capri is a block of limestone. The island has many caves, both at sea level and above, where water has worn away the rock. Old legends told of sea monsters lurking in a cave called the Grotta Gradola. In 1826, a German painter, August Kopisch, asked a Capri fisherman to take him to the cave in his boat. As Kopisch swam into the cave, he saw a striking blue light, and named it the Blue Grotto.

Tourists wait their turn to go into the Blue Grotto. In summer the average sea temperature here is a warm 26°C.

Sunlit water

You can sail into the cave through a low arch, just 1 metre above the surface of the sea. But the entrance to the cave is much larger, extending to 15 metres below the surface of the water. Sunlight enters the cave through the opening above the water and from below sea level. Light bounces off the sandy bottom of the cave, through the clear blue water, and lights up the rocky walls.

Today, the cave is a popular tourist attraction and is visited by many boats every day during the summer season.

FACTS

LENGTH	54 m
WIDTH	30 m
HEIGHT	15 m
WATER DEPTH	14-22 m
LOCATION	island of Capri, Italy

This photograph shows how the Blue Grotto got its name. A Roman **landing step** was found inside the cave, and the remains of a small Roman villa lie on the cliffs above.

In Roman times

People lived on Capri in prehistoric times, and the island later belonged to the Greeks and then the Romans. When the Roman emperor Tiberius lived there, he built 12 **villas**. He ruled the Roman Empire from the Villa Jovis from AD 27 to 37. Scientists believe that the Blue Grotto would have been the same then as it is now. In 1964 a number of Roman statues were found on the sea floor of the cave. These were taken to a museum on the island.

Carlsbad Caverns

This **system** of interconnecting caves lies beneath the surface of south-eastern New Mexico, in the United States. It contains some very large caves, or caverns. The largest cavern, called Big Room, is 550 metres long, 335 metres wide and up to 78 metres high. The region became a US **national park** in 1930.

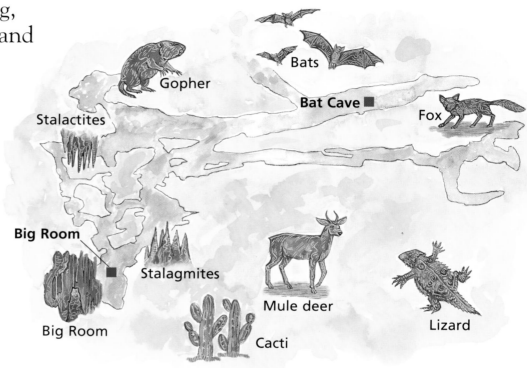

Gopher

Bats

Bat Cave ■

Fox

Stalactites

Big Room

Stalagmites

Mule deer

Lizard

Big Room

Cacti

This part of the Caverns is called the Dolls' Theatre. There is an **infrared** alarm system, which sounds if anyone touches the delicate rock formations.

Ancient limestone

Limestone is made up of the crushed skeletons of **corals** and other tiny sea creatures. The Carlsbad Caverns are carved out of a huge and ancient limestone formation. This limestone was once a coral reef, at the edge of an inland sea that covered the whole of New Mexico. Earth movements gradually lifted the limestone region above sea level and the sea water flowed away.

Stalactites and stalagmites

The Carlsbad Caverns are famous for their natural rock formations, which were formed by trickling water. Inside the caves, each droplet of water carries a tiny amount of dissolved limestone. The trickling droplets leave behind particles of limestone, and these slowly build up into formations called **speleothems**. The best-known speleothems are stalactites, which hang down like icicles, and stalagmites, which grow upwards. One Carlsbad cave contains what looks like a frozen waterfall. It is a cascade of stalactites.

FACTS

LENGTH OF CAVERNS	37 km
GREATEST DEPTH	309 m
CAVERN TEMPERATURE	13°C
AREA OF NATIONAL PARK	189 sq km
LOCATION	south-eastern New Mexico, USA

Some of the famous stalactites and stalagmites of Carlsbad, illuminated for visitors by electric lights. A complete tour through the Caverns takes about three hours.

Bat caves

In 1901 a New Mexico cowboy called Jim White saw a dark cloud rising from the ground ahead of him. When he went closer, he saw that the cloud was a swarm of bats. They were flying out of a hole in the ground. Jim came back the next day with a rope ladder and a lamp, to investigate. He discovered Carlsbad Caverns. Today, the caverns contain about half a million bats. Every evening, 5000 bats a minute zoom out of the caves to catch insects.

Eisriesenwelt

Eisriesenwelt means 'world of the ice giants' in German and is the name of the biggest system of ice caves in the world. The caves lie in the Tennengebirge, a range of mountains in the Austrian Alps. Tourists can visit the caves from May to October, from the ski resort of Werfen, 46 kilometres south of Salzburg.

Tennengebirge Mountains

Mountaineering

Ice formations

Eisriesenwelt

Ice veil

Alpine house

Cable cars

Snowboarding

Alpine cow

Skiing

Werfen ski resort

Hohenwerfen Castle

Visitors to Eisriesenwelt have a 15-minute walk from the top station of the cable railway to the entrance to the caves.

Icy world

The caves formed millions of years ago, when Europe's **climate** was warmer than it is now. Water gradually wore away cracks in the region's limestone rock to create caves. Today the climate is cooler and water freezes when it enters the caves. The temperature in the caves stays at **freezing point** all year so the icy formations never melt.

Alpine exploration

Local people have always known that there were caves in this region. The explorer Anton Posselt-Czorich found a large cave entrance in 1879. He went 250 metres into the cave and there he met a wall of ice. It was 34 years later, in 1913, when a caver called Alexander von Mörk managed to pass the ice wall. He discovered an enormous set of caves. Eisriesenwelt was opened to tourists in 1920. A vast cavern was named Mörk's Cathedral after the explorer who discovered it.

FACTS

LENGTH OF CAVES	42 km
ENTRANCE ALTITUDE	1641 m
CAVE TEMPERATURE	0°C
ICE AREA IN CAVES	30 000 sq m
LOCATION	Tennengebirge, Austria

Ice Giants

The caves' entrance leads to a 30-metre high wall of ice. Visitors climb up steps to the Posselt Gallery. **Magnesium** lights show up wonderful icy stalactites, stalagmites and columns of ice. These are called the Ice Giants. Other amazing ice formations have been given names such as Ice Organ, Ice Chapel and Ice Palace. The limestone caves go on for many kilometres beyond the tourist area.

The Ice Organ is one of the most impressive sights in Eisriesenwelt. On the opening day in 1920, 180 people walked all the way up the mountain to visit the caves.

Lascaux

The Lascaux cave is in the Dordogne region of south-west France. The cave is famous for its wonderful prehistoric paintings, which date back 17 000 years. These ancient paintings are found on the walls of the cave. They have helped us to learn about the lives of our human **ancestors**.

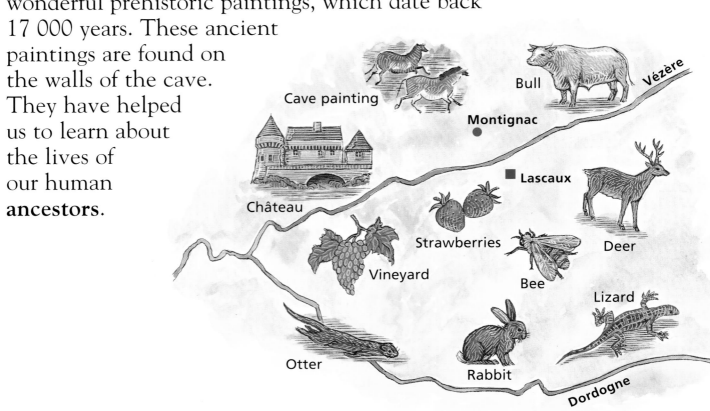

Cave painting

Bull

Vézère

Montignac

Château

Lascaux

Strawberries

Deer

Vineyard

Bee

Lizard

Otter

Rabbit

Dordogne

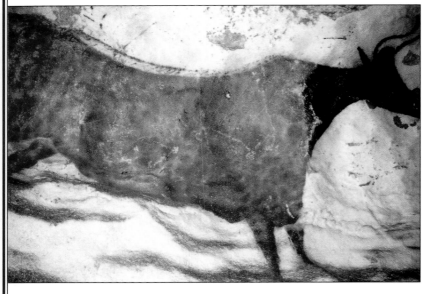

This red bull with a black head is on the wall of the Axial Gallery. There are more than 50 paintings of bulls at Lascaux.

Chance discovery

One day in 1940, four boys were walking through the woods on a hill near the town of Montignac. Their dog fell down a hole, and as they helped the dog out, the boys saw that the hole led to a large cave. They came back with an oil lamp, and were amazed to find the walls of the cave covered with paintings. The boys had discovered the cave that became the most famous prehistoric art gallery in the world.

FACTS

LENGTH OF CAVE	150 m
HALL OF BULLS	17 m long, 9 m wide, 5 m high
AXIAL GALLERY	20 m long, 1.5 m wide, 4 m high
NUMBER OF PAINTINGS	600
NUMBER OF ENGRAVINGS	1500
LOCATION	near Montignac, Dordogne, France

Prehistoric art

The cave has four galleries, but most
of the paintings appear in two of them:
the Hall of the Bulls and the Axial Gallery.
Many animals were painted and drawn on the walls, such as
an **extinct** bull called an aurochs. The biggest aurochs is over
5 metres long. There is also an animal with a single horn, that
looks like the legendary **unicorn**. Horses, deer, **ibexes**, bears
and woolly rhinoceroses also appear in these beautiful paintings.

Replica cave

Lascaux was opened to the public in
1948, but by 1963 two big problems had
arisen. Green **algae** and white limestone
deposits had started to appear on the
cave walls. These problems were caused
by millions of visitors who warmed the
cave and breathed carbon dioxide into
it. The cave had to be closed to save
the paintings. In 1973 work started on
a **replica** cave 200 metres away. Artists
copied the original pictures on the
replica limestone walls, and used the
same materials as their ancestors
thousands of years before. Lascaux II
opened in 1983.

The artist Monique Peytol painted copies
of the original works on to the walls of the
replica cave. She worked from photographs
and measurements of the original cave.

Lava Beds

This region of northern California, in the United States of America, contains hundreds of lava caves. There are many rock formations caused by ancient volcanoes and earthquakes. The area was made into a US national monument called Lava Beds in 1925.

TULE LAKE

Hawk

Rattlesnake

Pine forest

Kangaroo rat

Juniper tree

Black Crater

Owl

Marmot

Ground squirrel

Lava tube

Lava caves

Bald eagle

Mammoth Crater

Jack rabbit

FACTS

NUMBER OF CAVES	300+
HIGHEST POINT	1737 m
AREA OF NATIONAL MONUMENT	186 sq km
LOCATION	northern California, USA

Valentine Cave, one of the main caves at Lava Beds, is a good example of a lava tube. Visitors wear helmets and strong shoes to protect themselves from the sharp lava.

Caves in lava

Lava is molten rock thrown out by a volcano when it erupts. As it pours from the volcano, lava is very hot – almost 1000° C. The lava often cools and hardens on the outside, but stays hot and runny on the inside and goes on moving. The flow of lava inside the shell drains away, leaving a solid, hollow tunnel, or cave. There are more than 300 of these lava tubes at Lava Beds. Many formed about 30 000 years ago, after an eruption at nearby Mammoth **Crater**.

Modoc territory

For centuries this region was home to Modoc Indians. **Settlers** arrived in the 1850s and forced the Modocs to live on a **reservation** with other Native Americans who were their traditional enemies. The Modocs returned to their homeland, and in 1872 the US Army tried to round them up. The Modocs sheltered in the caves, and 52 warriors held off the Army for five months. In 1873, the Modoc leaders were killed and the rest were sent to a reservation in Oklahoma, 2000 kilometres away.

The black volcanic landscape above many of the caves was formed by an ancient lava flow. In the background is Schonchin Butte, a flat-topped hill made of layers of hard rock.

Jack rabbits and bald eagles

Most of the land surrounding Lava Beds is a wilderness. In the north of the region is grassland, in the middle are juniper trees and to the west is pine forest. The land is home to jack rabbits, ground squirrels, kangaroo rats and marmots, as well as rattlesnakes.

The jack rabbit is really a hare. It lives above ground and bounds along at up to 72 kilometres an hour. All these small mammals make ideal prey for the bald eagles that winter along the cliffs on Tule Lake. Other hunting birds in the area include hawks, falcons and owls.

Mammoth Cave

This huge **network** of caves lies under Mammoth Cave
National Park, in south-west Kentucky, USA. It forms
the longest system of connected caves in the world,
with a total mapped length of 560 kilometres.
The area became a national park in 1941.

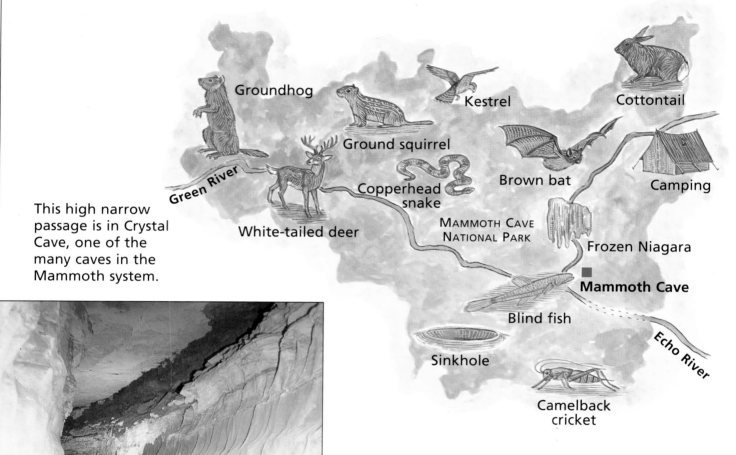

Groundhog

Kestrel

Cottontail

Ground squirrel

Green River

Copperhead
snake

Brown bat

Camping

White-tailed deer

MAMMOTH CAVE
NATIONAL PARK

Frozen Niagara

Mammoth Cave

Blind fish

Echo River

Sinkhole

Camelback
cricket

This high narrow
passage is in Crystal
Cave, one of the
many caves in the
Mammoth system.

Underground river

The fields around the national park are
full of **sinkholes**, some of which are more
than 30 metres deep. These sinkholes **funnel**
rainwater into the limestone caves below.
There are more than 250 cave entrances in
the national park, but only 30 of them lead
directly into Mammoth Cave. Green River
runs through the park, and one of its
tributaries, Echo River, runs through
Mammoth Cave, 110 metres below ground.

A guide throws a burning torch to light up a passage. This is a tradition in Mammoth Cave, first started by Indian explorers and nineteenth-century guides.

Using the caves

More than 10 000 years ago, groups of **Native Americans** wandered the Green River valley, hunting, fishing and gathering food. Around 3000 years ago, woodland Indians explored underground and searched the caves for minerals. European settlers arrived in the 1790s and **mined** the caves for **saltpetre**. By the 1840s, many people had started visiting the area and Mammoth Cave soon became a popular tourist attraction.

FACTS

LENGTH OF CAVES	560 km
GREATEST DEPTH	137 m
CAVE TEMPERATURE	12°C
AREA OF NATIONAL PARK	213 sq km
LOCATION	Kentucky, USA

Life in the dark

Some creatures spend their whole lives in Mammoth Cave. Many live in and around Echo River. There is no light so deep down, so these animals have pale pink, white or **translucent** skins, and some have no eyes. The blind **cavefish** has tiny sense bumps all over its body to help it find its way around. Eyeless, colourless cave crayfish and shrimps live in the dark underground river, and eyeless millipedes make their way along the damp, rocky walls of Mammoth Cave.

Naracoorte

Naracoorte Caves lie beneath a **conservation park** near the small rail town of Naracoorte, in South Australia. The caves are in a region of limestone hills, about 320 kilometres south-east of the **state capital** of Adelaide. Naracoorte takes its name from an **Aboriginal** word meaning 'large waterhole'.

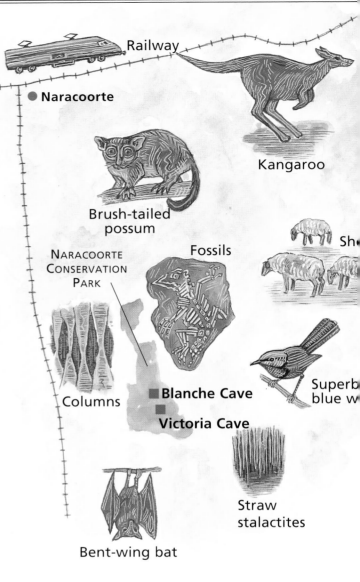

Railway

● Naracoorte

Kangaroo

Brush-tailed possum

NARACOORTE CONSERVATION PARK

Fossils

Sh

Columns

Blanche Cave

Victoria Cave

Superb blue w

Straw stalactites

Bent-wing bat

Spectacular stalactites and other formations make beautiful grottoes at Naracoorte. This one is called the Mirror Pool.

The Fossil Chamber

In 1845 a farm manager discovered caves here while searching for lost sheep. Fifty years later, a series of connecting **chambers** were discovered and named Victoria Cave. In 1969 three scientists found a narrow passage that led to another chamber, which they called Fossil Chamber. Here they found thousands of **fossilized** bones, the remains of prehistoric animals that died between 170 000 and 18 000 years ago. The Fossil Chamber was a truly amazing find.

Prehistoric meat-eater

Scientists have uncovered 93 different species of animals in the Fossil Chamber. The skulls, jaws and skeleton bones of frogs, turtles, snakes, lizards, birds and spiny anteaters were found here. The most famous finds were the bones of extinct **marsupials**, one of which was a marsupial lion. Scientists think this was a meat-eating animal, the size of a modern leopard. They believe the creature climbed trees, but hunted giant kangaroos and other **prey** on the ground.

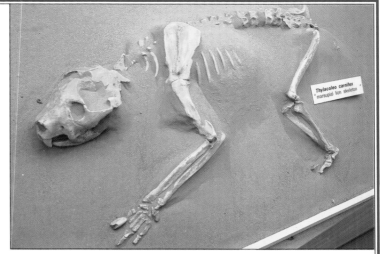

Naracoorte's skeleton of the marsupial lion.

FACTS

NUMBER OF CAVES	26
VICTORIA CAVE LENGTH	3 km
FOSSIL CHAMBER LENGTH	60 m
FOSSIL CHAMBER WIDTH	20 m
LOCATION	south-east Australia

Fun and adventure

Blanche Cave was one of the first caves to be discovered at Naracoorte. It has three large chambers, each with tall columns formed by stalactites joining up with stalagmites. In the 1850s, the local landowner held parties in the first chamber. He put in wooden benches, which are still there.

There are no wild parties there today, but visitors can go on an adventure tour instead. This gives them the exciting experience of exploring caves without electric lights, handrails or paths. A trained guide leads the visitors, as they crawl and slide their way through the dark tunnels and chambers.

Pierre-Saint-Martin

Pierre-Saint-Martin is one of the deepest caves in the world. It goes down 1.3 kilometres into the Pyrenees mountains, beneath the border between France and Spain. The cave's connecting passages measure more than 50 kilometres.

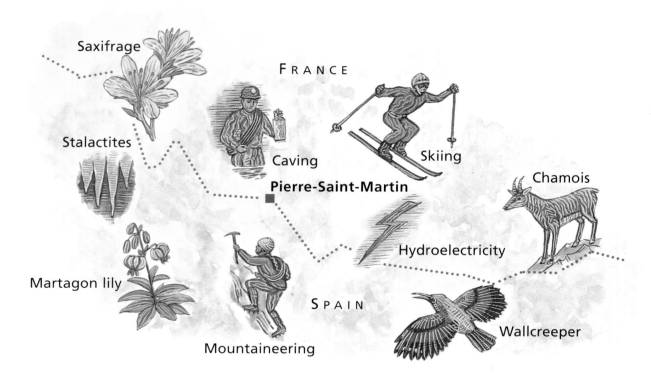

Saxifrage

Stalactites

Martagon lily

Caving

FRANCE

Pierre-Saint-Martin

Mountaineering

SPAIN

Skiing

Hydroelectricity

Chamois

Wallcreeper

Discovery

In August 1950 two cavers were walking across limestone rocks near the Pyrenean town of Arette-Pierre-St-Martin. Suddenly a bird flew up in front of them, from a hole in the rocks. One of the men, Georges Lépineux, returned in 1951 to explore the hole. It was a vertical **shaft**, 320 metres deep, with several passages leading from the bottom of it.

The beautiful Pyrenees mountain region where the cave was found.

Verna Chamber

In 1953 cavers discovered a huge chamber at a depth of 734 metres, a world record at the time. The Verna Chamber is 230 metres long, 180 metres wide and 150 metres high. Further passages were found leading off this, but the only way in was the vertical Lépineux entrance. Then a French electricity company dug a tunnel to the Verna Chamber to test its use for hydroelectricity – producing electricity by the force of flowing water. In 1965 another natural entrance was found higher up the mountain.

FACTS

DEPTH	1342 m
TOTAL LENGTH	52.2 km
HIGHEST ENTRANCE	2058 m
ARTIFICIAL TUNNEL LENGTH	700 m
LOCATION	France, Spain

Pierre-Saint-Martin is full of big passages and vertical shafts. In recent years more passages have been found to connect up with this deep cave system.

Sport and exploration

During the winter months, Arette-Pierre-St-Martin is a busy ski resort, and in the summer the area is full of cavers. Some go for fun, while others try to explore new passages. The cave is so popular that a special caving association decides which parties of cavers go down on which days. The original entrance has been blocked up, to prevent falls of rock, and in winter other entrances have wooden caps to stop snow from blocking them.

Sarawak Chamber

This is the largest known cave chamber in the world and it is found in the Malaysian state of Sarawak. Sarawak lies on the island of Borneo, in south-east Asia. The chamber forms part of a huge system of caves beneath Gunung Api, which means 'fire mountain'.
The rocky floor of Sarawak Chamber is big enough to hold 23 football pitches.

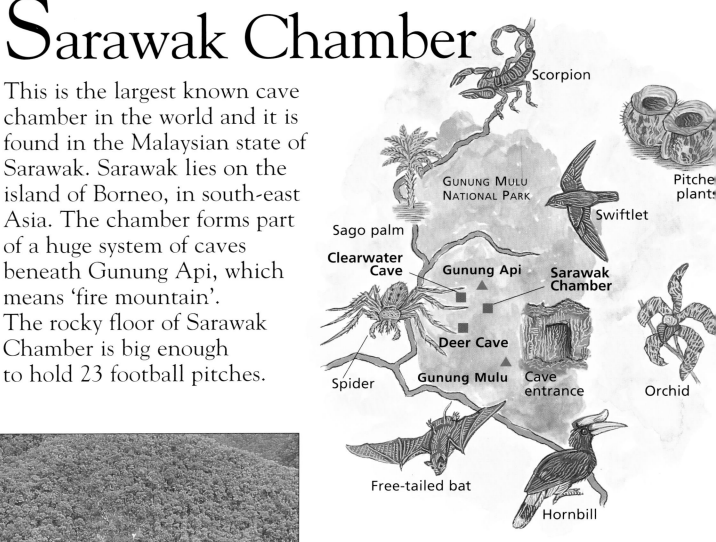

Scorpion

Pitcher plants

Gunung Mulu National Park

Swiftlet

Sago palm

Clearwater Cave

Gunung Api

Sarawak Chamber

Deer Cave

Spider

Gunung Mulu

Cave entrance

Orchid

Free-tailed bat

Hornbill

Gunung Mulu

The limestone mountain of Gunung Api is 1750 metres high. Nearby is an even higher mountain called Gunung Mulu, which rises to 2377 metres. Both Api and Mulu are more than 5 million years old. Gunung Mulu is the name of the national park that includes this whole area of mountains and caves. It was officially opened by Malaysia in 1985. The area is part of the homeland of the wandering Penan people, who traditionally gather food and nuts, harvest wild sago palms and hunt animals.

The entrance to Deer Cave is in a forested hill in Mulu National Park. It leads to a huge passage, close to the world's largest known cave chamber.

A fantastic discovery

Cavers started exploring caves in this area in 1974. They spent 10 years exploring and measuring 26 of the caves. But it was in 1980 that a group of explorers made a fantastic discovery. They were making their way along an underground passage, when they suddenly came upon a vast cavern. It was too big to be fully lit by their lamps, and it took them 12 hours to explore. The cavers had discovered the biggest cave chamber in the world. The chamber's amazing measurements are: 700 metres long, 300 metres wide, and between 70 and 120 metres from floor to ceiling.

Cavers light up just a small part of Sarawak Chamber. They continue to explore the region's caves, in the hope of finding an even bigger chamber.

FACTS

CHAMBER LENGTH	700 m
AVERAGE CHAMBER WIDTH	300 m
CHAMBER HEIGHT	70-120 m
NUMBER OF MULU CAVES	26+
LOCATION	Sarawak, Borneo, south-east Asia

Caves of Mulu

Since the Sarawak Chamber was discovered, explorers have mapped many more caves here, winding for a length of more than 200 kilometres beneath the national park. The Melinau River runs through the park, and its tributary, Clearwater River, flows underground through Clearwater Cave. Deer Cave has a passage 100 metres wide and 220 metres high. Swiftlets build their nests here, and poisonous scorpions, huntsman spiders, translucent crabs and white snakes live in the darkness of the caves.

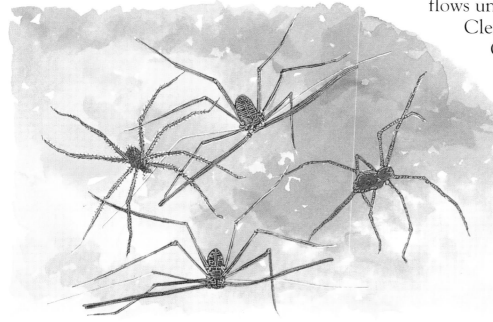

Waitomo

Waitomo Caves lie in a block of limestone near the west coast of New Zealand's North Island. They were explored in 1887 by a local Maori chief and an Englishman. The explorers soon discovered the caves' great natural wonders: beautiful limestone formations, and a grotto full of tiny pinpoints of light.

Fungus gnat

Maori carving

Glowworm threads

Tuatara lizard

Glowworm Cave

Cave weta

Limestone pillars

Aranui Cave

Ruakuri Cave

Waitomo River

Kiwi

Eucalyptus

Straw stalactites

Maori land

The Maoris are the original inhabitants of New Zealand. These Polynesian people sailed here from islands in the **mid-Pacific** a thousand years ago. In the Maori language, Waitomo means 'water running out of a hole' and the Waitomo River flows through the caves here. In 1989, the land and caves were returned to the Maori people. Tane Tinorau was the name of the Maori chief who first explored the caves. Some of the people who work at the caves today are Tane Tinorau's direct **descendants**.

A group of visitors enjoy the tour through Glowworm Cave and marvel at the thousands of points of light – all produced by insects.

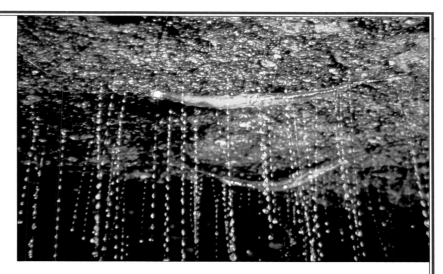
This close-up shows glowworm larvae with their sticky threads, which they use to catch insects.

Glowworm Cave

The first explorers saw thousands of bright blue lights when they entered Waitomo Caves. This light was made by glowworms on the cave's ceiling and walls. Glowworms are the larvae, or grubs, of tiny flies called fungus gnats. They produce light to attract other insects, which they trap in long, sticky threads that hang down like fishing lines. This type of glowworm lives only in New Zealand. Every year 250 000 people visit Waitomo Caves for a guided tour and boat ride through Glowworm Cave.

FACTS

LENGTH OF CAVES	85 km
HUMIDITY IN CAVES	94-99%
LONGEST STALACTITE	6 m
LONGEST STALAGMITE	3 m
LOCATION	North Island, New Zealand

Straws and columns

Waitomo has beautiful speleothems. Ruakuri Cave has straw stalactites which are 2 metres long. These speleothems are called straws because they have formed as hollow tubes and are only about 5 millimetres across.

Aranui Cave has thick limestone columns, or pillars, and delicate, curly formations called helictites, which grow on cave walls or stalactites. Some speleothems have a red, brown or green colour. This comes from minerals in the soil that wash through in rainwater.

The world's caves

There are amazing caves on all the world's continents. These include limestone caves in Africa and South America, and ice caves on the frozen continent of Antarctica. New caves are found and explored all the time.

Cango Caves

Cango Caves, in the Western Cape province of South Africa, are more than 3 kilometres long. We know from wall paintings that the caves were lived in by **Stone Age** people. The caves are famous for their wonderful limestone formations, including the Organ Pipes (right). Speleothems such as this are formed over thousands of years by water tracing a path down a cave wall, leaving behind particles of limestone.

Ice caves

Caves can form in ice, beneath **glaciers**, icebergs and ice sheets. This large ice cave (left) was photographed under a glacier in Antarctica, the frozen continent around the South Pole. Water flowing beneath the surface hollows out the ice caves. As the glaciers move, so do the caves, which constantly change shape and often collapse. Ice caves rarely last a long time.

Postojna Caves

The Postojna Caves (above) are in a region of Slovenia called Kras, or Karst. The word 'karst' is used to describe any limestone region with underground **channels** and a dry, barren surface. The Postojna Caves are famous for their beautiful formations, as well as a vast chamber known as the Concert Hall.

Cave of Windows

The Gruta do Janelao, or 'Cave of Windows' (left), has one of the largest cave passages in the world. It is 60 metres high and earned its name because holes in the roof let in light, like natural skylights or windows. This means that visitors can walk through the cave without using a torch. The Cave of Windows is in the Brazilian state of Minas Gerais, near the town of Januaria.

Glossary

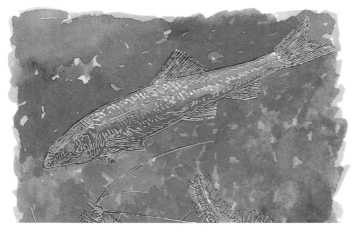

A cavefish swims in an underground river.

Aboriginal To do with Aborigines, the original people of Australia.

algae Tiny plants that grow in water or on damp surfaces.

ancestor A person from whom others are descended, through their parents, grandparents, and so on.

carbon dioxide A gas that makes up a tiny part of the air that we breathe.

cavefish A small fish that lives in underground streams and rivers.

chamber A large cave shaped like a room.

channel An underground stream or river.

climate A region's weather over a long time.

conservation park An area that people may visit where animals, plants and features such as caves are protected.

coral A tiny sea animal. Skeletons of many corals form a reef.

crater A bowl-shaped opening at the top of a volcano.

crust The Earth's outer shell.

deposit A build-up, such as that of limestone, over a period of time.

descendant A person who is the son (or daughter) grandson, great-grandson, and so on, of another person.

extinct An extinct animal is one that has completely died out.

formation (in caves) Shaped rocks and other features, such as stalactites.

fossilized Preserved (as the remains of prehistoric animals and plants).

Limestone formations in the Waitomo Caves.

freezing point The temperature at which water turns into ice (0°C).

funnel To let water pour through.

glacier A mass of ice that moves slowly like a river.

ibex A wild mountain goat.

infrared Referring to rays with a shorter wavelength than radio waves, such as those used by a TV remote control.

landing step A flat piece of rock used for stepping into and out of boats.

magnesium A silvery-white metal that burns with a bright flame.

marsupial An animal such as a kangaroo, koala or possum. Female marsupials carry their young in a pouch.

mid-Pacific The middle of the Pacific Ocean.

mine To dig for minerals.

molten Melted, turned into liquid.

national park An area that people may visit where animals, plants and features such as caves are protected.

Native American One of the original inhabitants of north America, also called Indians.

network A group of caves that connect up with each other.

prehistoric Relating to ancient times before writing was invented.

prey An animal that is hunted and killed by another animal for food.

replica An exact copy.

reservation An area of land set aside for American Indian people.

Prehistoric wall paintings at Lascaux.

saltpetre A natural white substance that is used to make gunpowder and fireworks.

settler A person who goes to live in a new country or region.

shaft A vertical underground passage.

sinkhole A funnel-shaped hole in the ground, where water flows into a cave.

speleothem A rock formation in a cave, such as a stalactite, caused by trickling water.

state capital The main city of a state, or separately-governed region.

Stone Age The prehistoric time when humans began to use stone tools.

system A large group of caves that connect up with each other.

translucent Almost see-through.

tributary A small river that flows into a larger one.

unicorn An imaginary animal that looks like a white horse with one long horn growing from its forehead.

Huntsman spiders in the Sarawak Chamber.

villa A country house.

Index

Words in **bold** appear in the glossary on page 30-31.